DELUXE ILLUSTRATED SONGBOOK

Blue Moo

17 *Jukebox Hits* FROM *Way Back Never*

> ## "BLUE MOO"
>
> **NAME** ▶ ◀ **NAME**
>
> ## "THIS BOOK BELONGS TO ME"

Lyrics and Drawings by Sandra Boynton

Music by Sandra Boynton & Michael Ford

Workman Publishing Company ☽ New York

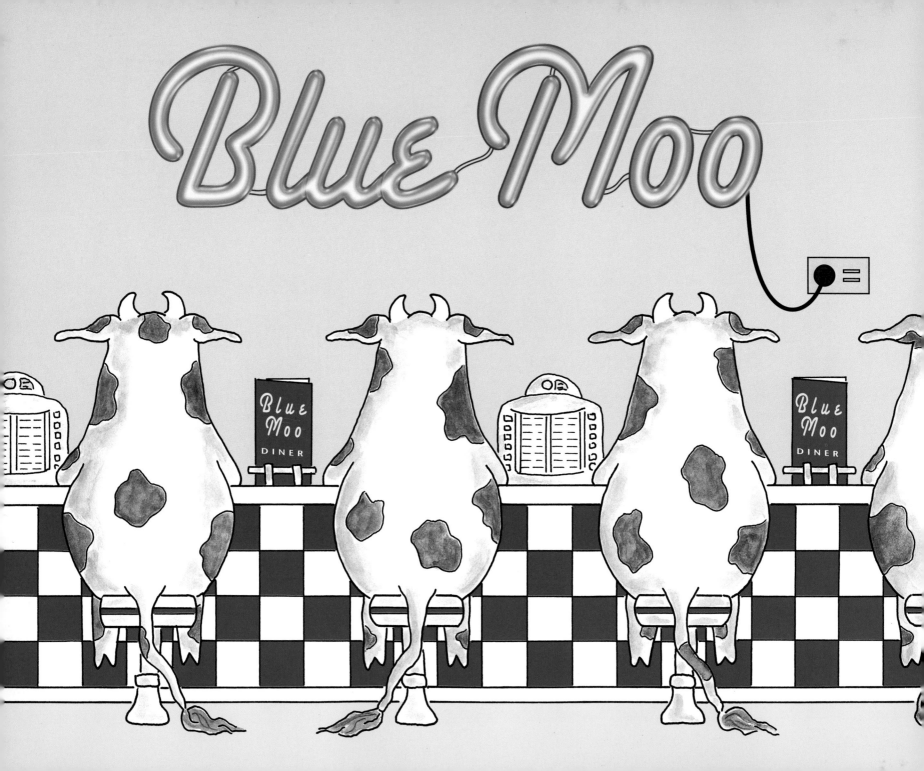

Today's Specials!

PART 1 LOOK WHILE YOU LISTEN . . . . *Page 3¢ through 38¢*   **RECORDING CREDITS** *Page 62¢*

PART 2 SING & PLAY ALONG . . . . *Page 39¢ through 54¢*   **THANK-YOUS** *Page 63¢*

PART 3 ABOUT THE SINGERS . . . . *Page 55¢ through 61¢*   **BOOK CREDITS** *Page 64¢*

Why not try Our HANDY cut-out INSERT *for Your* COMPACT DISC CASE**?** *Page 65¢*

Dedication

To the Magical Children in Our Lives

Caty, Keith, Devin, Darcy, Rae, John, Katie,
Zoë, Julianna, Christian, Spencer, Parker, Carson,
Katie, Elizabeth, Jack, Charlie, Madeline, Charlotte, Catherine, Alice, Ned,
Shawn, "B-Luc," Nina, Morgan, Chris,
Mabel, Kate, Jon, Chris,
Carnie, Wendy, Daria, Delanie, Dylan, Bo, Leo, Lola, Wendy's twins,
Marc, Dara, Amanda, Charlotte, Ethan Michael, Olivia, Johnny,
B. B. King's children, grandchildren, and great-grandchildren,
Jeff, Tommy, Robby, Jennifer, Bennett, Liam, Allison, Little Miss Vee 2 B,
Josh, Talia, Sarah, Jessica, Annabel, Harrison, Phoenix,
Victoria, Yvette-Louise, Thomas,
Kacie, Chris, Tommy, Lucie,
and Nina Y!

Recording and Book Ⓟ & © 2007 by Sandra Boynton   All rights reserved   No portion of this book or recording may be reproduced—mechanically, electronically, or by any other means, including photocopying and digital transfer—without written permission of the publisher and author   Published simultaneously in Canada by Thomas Allen & Son Limited
Songs with lyrics & music by Sandra Boynton are © SKBoynton Music   All other songs are © Boynton/Ford Music   All rights reserved   See page 62 for details
Library of Congress Cataloging-in-Publication Data is available
ISBN-13: 978-0-7611-4775-6
WORKMAN PUBLISHING COMPANY, INC. 225 Varick Street, New York, NY 10014-4381   www.workman.com   www.sandraboynton.com
The beautiful lake painting on page 12 is by Tina M. Campbell © 2007 Used by kind permission
First printing October 2007
10 9 8 7 6 5 4 3 2 1
Printed in Mexico

LOOK WHILE YOU LISTEN

Singing in the Shower! Singing in the Shower! I'm Singing in the Shower again!

Selection A-1

Singing in the Shower

Singing in the Shower! Singing in the Shower! Singing in the Shower!
I'm Singing in the Shower again!

Every morning when I wake up, well, my voice is all wrong.
You can hardly even hear me sing my song.
But I step into the shower. There's a whole new sound
as soon as the water's coming down.

Singing in the Shower! Singing in the Shower! Singing in the Shower!
I'm Singing in the Shower again!

Hey, the shiny silver sprayer makes a perfect microphone.
I could really be terrific with a band of my own.
I hear those back-up singers. Is it my imagination?
Just listen to that great reverberation!

(SINGING!) Oh, the mirror's getting foggy.
(SHOWER SINGING!) And the drums are getting soggy.
(SHOWER SINGING!) I'm happiest when
I'm Singing in the Shower again!

For Music and Full Lyrics kindly turn to Page 40

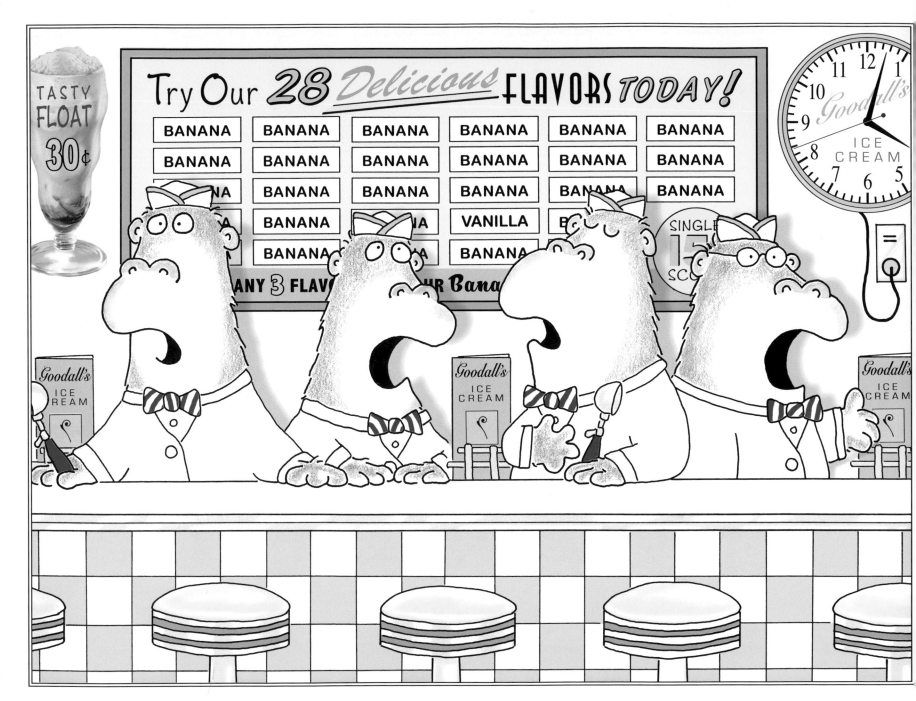

WE RECOMMEND! BANANA NANA NANA NANA NANA, NA NA NA.

Selection
A-2

Gorilla Song

BUHHHH-BUP! BANANA NANA.
BUHHHH-BUP! BANANA NANA. **BUHHHH-BUP!** BANANANA NANA.
BANANA NANA, NANA NANA, NANA NAH NAH! NUH NUH.

Bup. Bup. Banana! Bup. Bup. Banana! Bup...

BANANA NANA, NANA NANA, NA NA NA.
BANANA NANA, NANA NANA, NA NA NA.
BANANA NANA, NANA NANA, NA NA NA.
BUPBUP! BANANA NANA,
NANA NA NAH.

BUH! BUH!
NAH! NAH!
NUH! NUHHHHH!

For Music and Full Lyrics kindly turn to Page 41

It's sapphire and silver that's calling to you. Oh, the magic of the Blue, Blue Moo.

Selection
A-3

Blue Moo

Moo wop, moo wah. Moo wop, moooo wah. Moo wop, moo wah. Blue Moo wop, moo wah...

Have you ever heard a sound,
a melancholy air,
so distant you might wonder
if it's really even there?
It's something so simple,
and something so true—
the magic of the Blue, Blue Moo.

Have you ever been out drifting
in the twilight of the day
and something seemed to beckon,
though you couldn't really say?
It's sapphire and silver
that's calling to you.
Oh, the magic of the Blue, Blue Moo.

*For Music
and Full Lyrics
kindly turn to
Page 42*

MaRcHINg THRuUgH YuUR LIVINg RuuM!

...RuuM RuuM RuuM! AND THE BIG BASS DRuuM GOES RuuM!

WE ARE MARCHING THROUGH YOUR KITCHEN, FOR WE NEED A LITTLE SNACK.

Selection A-5

Return of the Uninvited Parade

WE ARE MARCHING THROUGH YOUR KITCHEN,
FOR WE NEED A LITTLE SNACK.
NOW WE ORGANIZE YOUR CUPBOARDS
AND WE EXIT OUT THE BACK.
WE'RE
THE UNINVITED LOUD PRECISION BAND!
IT'S THE BEST INTRUDING BAND
IN ALL THE LAND!

For Music and Full Lyrics kindly turn to Page 43

Now that turtle's always been a very peppy soul, and it gets around awfully quick.
But lately it's careening nearly out of control. I guess the four new sneakers give it extra kick.

Speed Turtle

I want to tell you of the most amazing thing I know.
You've got to just stand back now, and watch it go.
It is compact, streamlined, built to last,
shiny and green and so incredibly fast—

IT'S A... *SPEED TURTLE!* WHOA-HO!
IT'S A... *SPEED TURTLE!* OH, NO!
MAN ALIVE, IT'S IN OVERDRIVE. GO, LITTLE TURTLE, GO GO.

You know, it makes a little humming noise and moves like lightning.
Its superstock power is a little bit frightening.
And when that maniac gets going, well, hang on to your hat—
It can tear across the road in just three hours flat!

IT'S A... *SPEED TURTLE!* WHOA-HO!
IT'S A... *SPEED TURTLE!* OH, NO!
MAN ALIVE, IT'S IN OVERDRIVE. GO, LITTLE TURTLE, GO GO.

For Music
and Full Lyrics
kindly turn to
Page 44

You can tell everybody I told you so—It's the greatest little nose I know.

Selection A-7

Your Nose

Though I admire … Your Angel Eyes … There's something else … I idolize …

YOUR NOSE!
Oh whoa, whoa, whoa.
YOUR NOSE!
Whoa HOH! Ho.
It's got a magic I can't ignore.
What can I say? I just adore—

YOUR NOSE!
Oh whoa, whoa, whoa.
YOUR NOSE!
Whoa-oo-oh-OH!
It's the sweetest little thing.
Oh, can't you see?
No nose is like your nose
to me.

Now everyone can find a way
to happiness, I suppose.
When I am sad, I stop and gaze
at your amazing no-oo-oh-ose.

I love…
YOUR NOSE!
Oh whoa, whoa, whoa.
YOUR NOSE!
Whoa HOH! Ho.
You can tell everybody
I told you so—
It's the greatest little
nose
I know.

For Music and Full Lyrics kindly turn to Page 45

Do you wonder how a cow can touch your heart and soul?
*I don't know, but anyhow, it's what they call **Rock-and-Roll!***

Selection
A-8

Blue Moo '62

Tell me, have you heard a sound, sad and far away?
Maybe it is calling you. But who can ever say-ee-ay?
Is it really magic? Oh, this I know is true:
It's the Blue, Blue-hoo-oo Moo-oo.

Have you been out walking in the twilight of the day
and something seems to call your name,
but who can ever say-ee-ay-ee-ay?
When the song is silver, this I know is true:
It's the Blue, Blue-hoo-oo Moo-oo.

Do you wonder how a cow can touch your heart and soul?
I don't know, but anyhow, it's what they call

Rock-and-Roll!

For Music
and Full Lyrics
kindly turn to
Page 46

I WANT A SONG WITH A MELODY, RECORDED HIGH FIDELITY, OR BROADCAST LIVE. I WANT THE DRIVE.

Selection

Selection
A-9

BIG BAND SOUND

All alone…by the microphone. And dreaming—

I! want! a **BIG BAND SOUND.** I want a big…**BAND** sound.
I! want! a **BIG BAND SOUND.** I want a big…**BAND** sound.
I! want! a **BIG BAND SOUND.** I want a big…**BAND** sound.
I! want! a **BIG BAND SOUND.** I want a big…**BAND** sound.
I want **SAXOPHONES.** I want **SLIDE TROMBONES.**
I want **TRUMPETS** and **BASS** all around.
I want the jazz. **Pizzazz.** The razzamatazz—
I want the…sound.

For Music and Full Lyrics kindly turn to Page 47

I've got the One Shoe Blues. It seems they're never gonna stop.
Yes, those One Shoe Blues. Oh, they might not ever ever stop.

Selection A-10

One Shoe Blues

Well, I woke up this morning.
Couldn't find my shoe.
Yes, I woke up this morning,
and I
couldn't find my shoe.
Although the right one is here,
I need the left one, too.
(Yes, I do.)

I can hear my mama calling.
She says it's time to go.
Yes, I can hear my mama calling.
She says:
**REALLY NOW.
IT'S TIME TO GO.**

I say:
Mama, I can't find one of my shoes!
And she says:
OH, NO. NOT AGAIN.

I've got the One Shoe Blues.
It seems they're never gonna stop.
Yes, those One Shoe Blues.
Oh, they might not ever ever stop.

Mama says:
JUST COME ON ALONG NOW!

One shoe...
Do you expect me
to hop?

For Music and Full Lyrics kindly turn to Page 48

I want to be with you whenever I can.

With You

I want to be with you
whenever I can.
Just to walk with you.
Just to talk with you.
Just holding your hand.

I want to be near you
to hear what you may say.
Knowing more of you,
so adoring you.
Oh! Every way.

To **BE**...   spending time with you.
ME...   oh so fine with you.
GEE!   Knowing
I'm with you

day by day.

And
WHEN...
I'm apart from you
THEN...
goes my heart with you.
So! I'll wait! Till when—
we're back together,
and ever again.

For Music
and Full Lyrics
kindly turn to
Page 49

LOTS OF PEOPLE! [Only me.] **LOTS OF PEOPLE! LOTS OF PEOPLE!** [Only only me.]

Selection A-12

LOUD! / QUIET

LOUD LOUD LOUD! QUIET QUIET QUIET. LOUD LOUD LOUD! QUIET QUIET QUIET.

LOUD LOUD, LOUD LOUD! QUIET QUIET QUIET.

LOUD LOUD LOUD! QUIET QUIET QUIET.

LOTS OF PEOPLE! (Only me.)

LOTS OF **PEOPLE!** LOTS OF **PEOPLE!** (Only only me.)

REALLYREALLYFAST. REALLYREALLYFAST.
REALLYREALLYREALLYREALLYREALLYREALLY
FAST.

Slowwwwwwwwwww......

For Music and Full Lyrics kindly turn to Page 50

Now with that rabbit as if by habit you begin that thrilling dance across the floor,
while in the hot light of your own spotlight there's a magic that you never knew before.

Rabbit Tango

¿Quieres sentir lo que es vivir? El **TANGO...**

If there's a rabbit,
then you should grab it.
Then you should grab it,
gently nab it,
by the paws.
And then sincerely
you hold it nearly
as you await the sudden hush,
and then applause.

Now with that rabbit
as if by habit
you begin that thrilling dance
across the floor,
while in the hot light
of your own spotlight
there's a magic that you
never knew
before.

For *Bingo-Bango*! It is a **TANGO**!
You hear the violins above
and bass beneath.
It is dramatic. It's *SO* dramatic,
as the bunny holds a rose
between its teeth.

¡Oh!—¿Quieres bailar?
Oh, la noche. Oh, la música. Ah si.
¡Ay!—¿Quieres soñar?
Las estrellas y un conejo están aqui.

(Do you want to dance?)

If there's a rabbit,
then you should grab it.
Then you should grab it,
gently nab it, as it were.
But if there's not one,
you haven't got one,
and so the tango that we spoke of
won't occur.

*For Music
kindly turn to
Page 51*

When a Hippo Can Dance, it's a thrilling revelation.

Selection A-15

When a Hippo Can Dance

If you have a hippo you love very much,
yet you find it has one or two faults—
such as sleeping too late,
such as making you wait—
I suggest that you teach it to waltz.

Now, there may be a lot of us
who think: "HIPPOPOTAMUS"
and don't picture musical grace.
But just offer the chance to experience dance,
and you may be surprised what takes place.

When a Hippo Can Dance, it's a thrilling revelation.
When a Hippo Can Dance, there is nothing to say.
When a Hippo Can Dance, it's an overnight sensation.
Don't delay. Teach your hippo today.

For Music and Full Lyrics kindly turn to Page 52

I want to be Your Personal Penguin. I want to talk with you, night and day.
I want to be Your Personal Penguin. I want to listen to whatever you say.

Selection A-16

Your Personal Penguin

I like you a lot. You're funny, and kind. So let me explain what I have in mind...

I want to be your
☆ PERSONAL PENGUIN! ☆
I want to walk right by your side.
I want to be your
☆ PERSONAL PENGUIN! ☆
I want to travel with you, far and wide.
Wherever you go, I'll go there, too.
Here and there and everywhere, and always with you.
I want to be your
☆ PERSONAL PENGUIN! ☆
from now on.

For Music and Full Lyrics kindly turn to Page 53

May you always hear as you fall asleep a Mersey Lullaby. A Mersey Lullaby.

Selection
A-17

Mersey Lullaby

ome. Come on along.
Can you hear the river song?
Far away the river.
Far away that song
in the dark and endless sky.
I can almost hear in my memory
a Mersey Lullaby.

Now the day is done.
Gone away the golden sun.
Far away the river.
Far away that song,
and I sometimes wonder why
I can almost hear in my memory
a Mersey Lullaby.

Yes, I know it's been
a long and lovely day.
It's not easy now to let it go.
But, oh, my darling,
let it fade away.
Gently dream until tomorrow.

Here and everywhere,
is there music
in the air?
Far away the river.
Far away that song
in the dark and endless sky.
May you always hear
as you fall asleep
a Mersey Lullaby.
A Mersey Lullaby.

Come.
Come on along.

(Lullaby. Lullaby.)

Gone away the sun.

(Lullaby. Lullaby.)

Music everywhere.

(Lullaby. Lullaby.)

Oh—everywhere.

Lullaby.

For Music kindly turn to Page 54

"*We're on parade. We're on parade.*
Just when you thought this record was all through.
A swell brigade. We're on parade. We are back once more. Wuh-ho! *It's true.*
And we'll sing all night to you.

We are here below your window. We suspect you need your rest.
But we have some things to tell you, though by now you may have guessed:
We're the Uninvited Loud Precision Band. *It is the best.*
(*IT'S THE BEST INTRUDING BAND IN ALL THE LAND.*)
It's the BEST INTRUDING BAND! In all…the LAND!!!!!"

SING & PLAY ALONG

Selection A-1

Singing in the Shower

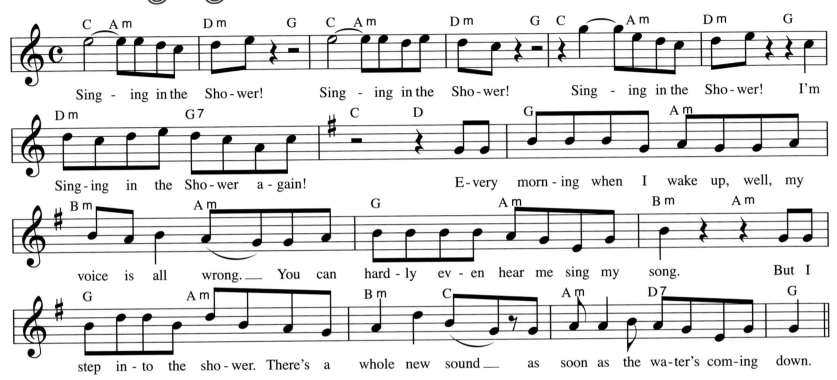

Sing - ing in the Sho - wer! Sing - ing in the Sho - wer! Sing - ing in the Sho - wer! I'm

Sing - ing in the Sho - wer a - gain! E - very morn - ing when I wake up, well, my

voice is all wrong. ___ You can hard - ly ev - en hear me sing my song. But I

step in - to the sho - wer. There's a whole new sound ___ as soon as the wa - ter's com - ing down.

Singing in the Shower! Singing in the Shower!
Singing in the Shower!
I'm Singing in the Shower again!

Hey, the shiny silver sprayer
makes a perfect microphone.
I could really be terrific
with a band of my own.
I hear those back-up singers.
Is it my imagination?
Just listen to that great reverberation!

(SINGING!)
Oh, the mirror's getting foggy.
(SHOWER SINGING!)
And the drums are getting soggy.
(SHOWER SINGING!)
I'm happiest when
I'm Singing in the Shower again.

I like the shimmer of the tile
and the rhythm like rain.
When the new day comes,
I've just got to entertain.
I bring so much emotion
to **EV-E-RY SIN-GLE RE-FRAIN!**

...It's a shame to see this talent
going right down the drain.

Now, some day I may be singing
whoa! in Carnegie Hall
and you know that I'll be bringing,
yeah, my own shower stall.
We're wearing waterproof tuxedos.
(MAYBE PURPLE SATIN SPEEDOS)
or I'm not singing there at all.

Singing!
And in the big finale
Singing!
I sound
JUST LIKE FRANKIE VALLI!
Singing! I-yi-yi-yi-yi'm
Singing in the Shower again!

Oh, I! I like to sing high!
But I! get cold by and by.
Now I! just want to be dry.
Singing in the Shower.
Singing in the Shower.
Singing in the Shower.
Singing in the Shower.
Singing in the Shower.
Singing in the Shower.
Singing in the Shower.
*Sing...*THANK YOU.

Gorilla Song

*B*uhhhh-bup! Banana nana.
Buhhhh-bup! Banana nana.
Buhhhh-bup! Bananana nana.
Banana nana, nana nana, nana nah nah! Nuh nuh.

(BUP. BUP. BANANA! BUP. BUP. BANANA! BUP...)

BA - NA-NA NA-NA NA-NA NA-NA, NA NA NA. BA - NA-NA NA-NA NA-NA NA-NA,

NA NA NA. BA - NA-NA NA-NA NA-NA NA-NA, NA NA NA. BUP-BUP! BA-NA-NA NA-NA. NA-NA NA NAH.

BUH! BUH! NAH! NAH! NUH! NUHHH!

**BANANA NANA NANA NANA,
NA NA NA.
BANANA NANA NANA NANA,
NA NA NA.
BANANA NANA NANA NANA,
NA NA NA.
BUPBUP! BANANA NANA.
BUPBUP! BANANA NANA.
BUPBUP! BANANA NANA.
NANA NA NAH.**
Ooooo—

[Solo:]
BaNAHna na NAHna,
NAH na na.
Banana nana nana nana,
na na na.
BaNAHna, NAHna, NAH na na.
Banana na NAH na,
banana NAH nahhh!

BUH! NAH! NUH!
Banana NAna.
SHA! NA! NA!
Banana NAna.

BUH! NAH! NUH!
Bananana NAna.
Bup! Banana.
Bup! Banana.
Bup! Bup! Banana.
Bup! Bup! Bup!
Banana.
Ohhhhhh!
We Recommend:
**BANANA NANA NANA NANA,
NA NA NA.
BANANA NANA NANA NANA,**

**NA NA NA.
BANANA NANA NANA NANA,
NA NA NA.
BUPBUP! BANANA NANA.
BUPBUP! BANANA NANA. BUP!**

Now, your average gorilla
may be wild about vanilla,
but I'd have to say banana
is my favorite food.
BADIDDLY BOP BANANA NANA,
NANA NA NAH!
Ooo!

Blue Moo

Moo wop, moo wah. Moo wop, moooo wah. Moo wop, moo wah, Blue Moo wop, moo wah...

Have you e-ver heard a sound, _____ a mel-an-cho-ly air, _____ so dis-tant you might won-der if it's

real - ly _____ e - ven there?   It's some-thing _____ so sim-ple, and some-thing _____ so true.   The

ma - gic of the Blue, Blue   Moo _____ oo.   Have you e-ver been out drif-ting _____ in the

twi-light of the day _____ and some-thing _ seemed to bec-kon, though you could - n't real - ly say?   It's

sap - phire _ and sil - ver   that's call-ing to you.   Oh, the ma-gic of the Blue, Blue   Moo. _____

Now, how can a cow that no one ever sees
play a song that makes you stand still?
How can it be that no one but she
seems to understand what nobody will?
It's a new kind of blue kind of mesmerizing tune.
Oh, a low kind of slow kind of saxophone croon.
It's the right kind of night kind of dark side of the moon.
It's a strong kind of song kind of...
come and gone too soon.

Have you ever heard a sound,
a melancholy air,
so distant you might wonder
if it's really even there?
It's something so simple,
and something so true.
It's the magic of the
Blue, Blue Moo-ooo-ooo.
The magic of the Blue, Blue Moo.

The Uninvited Parade

Selection A-4

WE'RE ON PAR-ADE! WE'RE ON PAR-ADE! WE ARE

MARCH-ING, MARCH-ING THROUGH YOUR LIV-ING ROOM! A SWELL BRI-GADE! WE'RE ON PAR-ADE!

AND THE BIG BASS DRUM GOES BOOM BOOM BOOM! AND THE BIG BASS DRUM GOES BOOM!

WE ARE MARCHING UP THE STAIRS. WE ARE MARCHING DOWN THE HALL. WE WILL HAVE TO TURN AROUND BECAUSE
YOUR HALLWAY IS TOO SMALL. PARADE! WE'RE ON PARADE! WE ARE MARCHING THROUGH YOUR CLOSET, UNAFRAID!
WE ARE MARCHING DOWN THE STAIRS. WE ARE MARCHING OUT THE DOOR. WE WILL SING OUR NOBLE ENDING JUST LIKE
EVERY TIME BEFORE: WE'RE THE UNINVITED LOUD PRECISION BAND! IT'S THE BEST INTRUDING BAND IN ALL THE LAND!

Selection A-5

Return of the Uninvited Parade

WE ARE MARCHING THROUGH YOUR KITCHEN, FOR WE NEED A LITTLE SNACK.
NOW WE ORGANIZE YOUR CUPBOARDS, AND WE EXIT OUT THE BACK.
WE'RE THE UNINVITED LOUD PRECISION BAND! IT'S THE BEST INTRUDING BAND IN ALL THE LAND!

The Uninvited Parade Strikes Again

Selection A-14

WE'RE ON PARADE! WE'RE ON PARADE! WE ARE MARCHING, MARCHING THROUGH THE GROCERY STORE!
A SWELL BRIGADE! WE'RE ON PARADE! AND THE BIG BASS DRUM GOES BOOM SOME MORE! AND THE DRUM GOES BOOM SOME MORE!
WE ARE MARCHING UP ROW A. WE ARE MARCHING DOWN ROW B. WE ARE MARCHING UP ROW C. WE ARE... [ETC. THROUGH ROW Z]
PARADE! WE'RE ON PARADE! WE ADMIRE HOW YOUR PRODUCE IS DISPLAYED!
WE HAVE MARCHED THROUGH EVERY AISLE OF THIS CROWDED SUPERMART.
WE ARE MARCHING THROUGH THE CHECKOUT LANE WITH NOTHING IN OUR CART!
WE'RE THE UNINVITED LOUD PRECISION BAND! IT'S THE BEST INTRUDING BAND IN ALL THE LAND!

Blue Moo

Speed Turtle

I want to tell you of the most a-maz-ing thing I know. _____ You've got to

just stand back now, and watch it go. _____ It is com-pact, stream-lined, built to last, _____

shi-ny and green and so in-cre-di-bly fast. _____ It's a... Speed Tur-tle. Whoa - ho! _____ It's a...

Speed Tur-tle. Oh, no! _____ Man a-live, it's in o-ver-drive. _____ Go, lit-tle tur-tle, go go. _____

(HARD TOP NONSTOP FOUR-ON-THE-FLOOR.)

You know,
it makes a little humming noise
and moves like lightning.

(MOVES LIKE LIGHTNING!

MOVES LIKE LIGHTNING!)

Its superstock power
is a little bit frightening.

(GO, SPEED TURTLE! GO, SPEED TURTLE!)

And when that maniac gets going,
well, hang on to your hat—
It can tear across the road in just

three hours flat!
It's a... Speed Turtle. Whoa-ho!
It's a... Speed Turtle. Oh, no!
Man alive, it's in overdrive.
Go, little turtle, go go.

Now that turtle's always been
a very peppy soul,
and it gets around awfully quick.
But lately it's careening nearly
out of control.
I guess the four new sneakers
give it extra kick.

(EXTRA KICK!)

Well, I don't know why
that turtle
keeps on pushing the pace now.

(DIH DIDDIT DIH DIT! PUSHING THE PACE!)

Every minute of the day is like
some kind of race now.

(SOME! KIND! OF RACE!)

With a gotta-get-there attitude
that never fails,
it blazes right past
EVERY ONE OF US SNAILS!

(ALL OVER TOWN, IT'S GONNA SHUT US DOWN.)

It's a... Speed Turtle.
Whoa-ho!
It's a... Speed Turtle.
Oh, no!
Man alive,
it's in overdrive.
So go, little turtle, go go.
Yeah, go, little turtle, go go.
Let's go, little turtle, go go.
Come on and go, little turtle, go go.
Get down and go, little turtle, go go.
I said now go, little turtle, go go.
It's time to go, little turtle, go go...

Selection
A-7

Your Nose

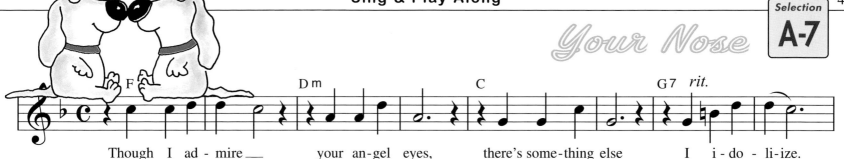

Though I ad - mire___ your an-gel eyes, there's some-thing else I i - do - li - ize.

YOUR NOSE!___ Oh whoa, whoa, whoa. YOUR NO - OSE! Whoa hoh! Ho.___ It's got a ma-gic I

can't ig-nore.__ What can I say?_ I just a-dore__YOUR NOSE!_ Oh whoa, whoa, whoa. YOUR NO - OSE!

Whoa - oo oh OH!___ It's the sweet-est lit-tle thing. Oh, can't you see?__ No nose is like your__ nose to me.___

Now everyone can find a way
to happiness, I suppose.
When I am sad, I stop and gaze
at your amazing no-oo-oh-ose.

I love
YOUR NOSE!
Oh whoa, whoa, whoa.
YOUR NOSE! Whoa HOH! Ho.
You can tell everybody
I told you so—It's the
greatest little nose I know.

Well, everyone can find a way
to happiness, I suppose.

When I am sad, I stop. And gaze.
At your amazing no-oo-oh-ose.
Ahhhhh—[CHOO!] *Bless you and*
YOUR NOSE!
Oh whoa, whoa, whoa.
YOUR NOSE!
Uh wuh-HOH! Ho.
It's the cutest little thing, and
heaven knows
no nose is like your nose to me.

YOUR NOSE!
Oh whoa, whoa, whoa.
YOUR NOSE!
Whoa HOH! Ho.

(YOUR NOSE.)
That nose is looking good.
(YOUR NOSE.)
Best nose in the neighborhood.
(YOUR NOSE.)
Oh, baby, I've got to say—
(YOUR NOSE.)
best nose in the U.S.A.
(YOUR NOSE.)
I love that nose because...
(YOUR NOSE.)
it's the best that ever was.
(YOUR NOSE.)
Best nose in the galaxy.
(YOUR NOSE.)

Best nose there could ever be.
(YOUR NOSE.)
Oh whoa, whoa, whoa.
Your nose.
Your adorable nose.
Oh whoa, whoa, whoa.
Your nose.
Oh! Uh wuh-HOH! Ho.
Your nose!
Oh whoa, whoa, whoa.
Your nose.
Such an excellent nose!
Oh whoa, whoa, whoa.
Your nose...

Selection
A-8

Blue Moo '62

Oo, ooo!
Oo, ooo!

Tell me, have you heard a sound, _____ sad and far a - way? _____ May - be it is

call - ing you. _____ But who can e - ver say - ee - ay? _____ Is it real - ly mag - ic? Oh,

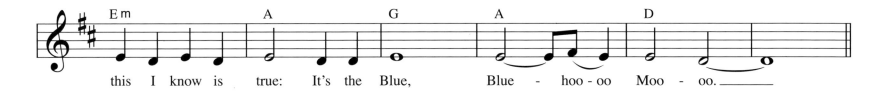

this I know is true: It's the Blue, Blue - hoo - oo Moo - oo. _____

Have you been out walking
in the twilight of the day
and something seems to
call your name,
but who can ever
say-ee-ay-ee-ay?
When the song is silver,
this I know is true:
It's the
Blue, Blue-hoo-oo Moo-oo.

Do you wonder how a cow
can touch your heart and soul?
I don't know, but anyhow,
it's what they call *ROCK-AND-ROLL!*

[SAX SOLO]

Do you wonder how a cow
can touch your heart and soul?
I don't know, but anyhow
it's what they call *ROCK-AND-ROLL!*

Oh, tell me,
have you heard a sound,
sad and far away?
Maybe it is calling you.
But who can ever say-ee-ay?
Is it really magic?
Oh, this I know is true:
It's that ooooo—Blue Moo.
That ooooo—Blue Moo.
That ooooo—Blue Moo.

Blue-ooo-oooo, ooo, Blue Moo. Blue-ooo-oooo...

Big Band Sound

HEY, ARE YOU RECORDING?
All alone by the microphone. TESTING. *And dreaming…*

SPOKEN OR SUNG

X 3

I! ___ want! a Big Band Sound. I want a big… BAND sound. I! ___ want! a

Big Band Sound. I want a big… BAND sound. I want sax-o-phones. I want slide trom-bones. I want

trum-pets and bass ___ all a-round. ___ I want the jazz. Pizz-azz. The razz-a-ma-tazz. ___ I want the… sound.

I! want! a Big Band Sound. I want a big…BAND sound.
I! want! a Big Band Sound. I want a big…BAND sound.

Now I know you maybe think I'm not the logical choice.
I am a rock-and-roll singer with a rock-and-roll voice.
But everything I wanted has now suddenly changed:
I want music that can be arranged.

…and a 1, 2, 3, 4…

I! want! a Big Band Sound. I want a big…BAND sound.

I play ironic retro rock with only three other guys.
But I'm thinking of a band of significant size.
I want a big band leader and a blue, blue moon.
I want to…croon?

I! want! a Big Band Sound. I want a big…BAND sound.

My heart belongs to rock-and-roll,
but swing belongs to my soul. Yes.

I want a song with a melody for me to sing.
I want that true, high fidelity, Big Band swing.

I want to move the song along, make it seem so easy—
So sincere, a little dark and breezy.

I! want! a Big Band Sound. I want a big…BAND sound.

I want the sass. The brass. The undeniable class.

…a big…BAND sound.

I've been a lo-fi guy, but I don't really care,
I want extravagant sound from the Big Band Era, want
a song with a melody
recorded high fidelity
or broadcast live.
I want the drive.

Downshift.

And when I get to the end of the big band story,
let me savor every word in its big band glory.
Want to bring it on home. I want to slow it all down.
I want a—wait for it—
BIG. BAND. Sound.

One Shoe Blues

Well, I woke up this morn - ing. ____ Could-n't find ____ my shoe.

Yes, I woke up this morn - ing, and I could-n't find my shoe.

Al-though the right one is here, ____ I need the left one, too. (Yes, I do.)

I can hear my mama calling.
She says it's time to go.
Yes, I can hear my mama calling.
She says:
REALLY now, it's time to go.
I say:
MAMA, I CAN'T FIND ONE OF MY SHOES!
And she says: **Oh, no. Not again.**

I've got the One Shoe Blues.
It seems they're never gonna stop.
Yes, those One Shoe Blues.
Oh, they might not ever ever stop.
Mama says:

Just come on along now!
One shoe.
Do you expect me to hop?

**Did you look in the closet
and under the bed?**
YES, I DID.
**Did you look
C A R E F U L L Y
in the closet and under the bed?**
YES, YES, I DID.
Try and think where you left it.
That's what my mama said.

Last night I left it right here
next to my other shoe.
I KNOW I put it right here
next to my other shoe.
I think somebody took it.
But I don't know who.
NO, I DON'T.

I've got the
One Shoe Blues.
That's why I'm singing this song.
I've got the
One Shoe Blues!
And so I'm singing this sad song.

You know it's been
at least twenty minutes
that I've been looking
in every POSSIBLE place
for that …

HUH.

THERE IT IS.

I guess it was on my foot
all along.

OKAY, I'M READY TO GO NOW.

ANYBODY SEEN MY COAT?

With You

I want — to be with you when-e-ver I can. Just to walk — with you.

Just to talk — with you. Just! hold-ing your hand. I want to be near you — to

hear what — you may say. Know-ing more — of you, so a-dor-ing you. Oh! E-ver-y way.

To **BE...** (WITH YOU!)
spending time with you.
ME... (WITH YOU!)
oh so fine with you.
GEE! (WITH YOU!)
Knowing I'm with you
day by day.
And **WHEN** (OH, NO!)
I'm apart from you
THEN (HOH!)
goes my heart with you.
So! I'll wait! Till when—
we're back together
and ever again!

For
I want to be with you
whenever I can.
Just to walk with you.
Just to talk with you.
Just!
a-holding your hand.
I want to be near you
to hear
what you may say.
Knowing more of you,
so adoring you,
(OH!)
in every way.

To **BE...** (WITH YOU!)
spending time with you
ME... (WITH YOU!)
oh so fine with you
GEE! (WITH YOU!)
Knowing I'm with you,
day by day.

And, oh!
I just want you to know
everywhere that you go
my love is always with you.
Wuh! a ho ho!
Is always with you...

Blᴜᴇ Mᴏᴏ

Loud! / Quiet

LOUD LOUD LOUD! ___ (Qui - et qui - et qui - et.) LOUD LOUD LOUD! ___ (Qui - et qui - et qui - et.)

LOUD LOUD, LOUD LOUD! (Qui - et qui - et qui - et.) LOUD LOUD LOUD! ___ (Qui - et qui - et qui - et.)

LOTS of PEO - PLE! (On - ly me.) Lots of PEO-PLE! Lots of PEO-PLE! (On-ly on-ly me.)

REAL-LY REAL-LY FAST. REAL-LY REAL-LY FAST. REAL-LY REAL-LY REAL-LY REAL-LY REAL-LY REAL-LY FAST. (Slowwwwww. . . . . .)

LOUD LOUD LOUD! Quiet quiet quiet.
LOUD LOUD LOUD! Quiet quiet quiet.
LOUD LOUD, LOUD LOUD! Quiet quiet quiet.
LOUD LOUD LOUD! Quiet quiet quiet.
FAR AWAY! Vᴇʀʏ ɴᴇᴀʀ.
FAR AWAY! Sᴏ ᴠᴇʀʏ ɴᴇᴀʀ. Qᴜɪᴇᴛ, Qᴜɪᴇᴛ.
LOUD LOUD LOUD! Qᴜɪᴇᴛ, Qᴜɪᴇᴛ.
LOUD LOUD LOUD!
Oh, lots of people! Only…Only me! Only me! So small!

SO BIG. So small!
SO BIG. SO BIG. SO BIG AND LOUD LOUD…

LOUD LOUD LOUD! Quiet quiet quiet.
LOUD LOUD LOUD! Quiet quiet quiet.
LOUD LOUD, LOUD LOUD!

OVER TO THE LEFT.
OVER TO THE LEFT.
REALLYREALLYFAST.
SINGINGTHESEWORDSSOFAST
YOUCANHARDLYUNDERSTANDASINGLE
THINGI'MTRYINGTOSAY!

Slowwwwwwwwww…Yup.

STOMP STOMP STOMP STOMP! Tippy tippy toes.
STOMP STOMP STOMP STOMP! Tippy tippy toes.
STOMP STOMP STOMP STOMP! Tippy tippy toes.
STOMP STOMP STOMP STOMP! Tippy tippy toes.

OVER TO THE LEFT.
OVER TO THE LEFT.

OVER TO THE RIGHT.
OVER TO THE RIGHT.
REALLYREALLYFAST.

OVER TO THE RIGHT.
OVER TO THE RIGHT.

Up high! **DOWN LOW.**
Up high! **DOWN LOW.**

Feeling somewhat melancholy. O.

Sad sad sad. Happy happy happy!
Sad sad sad. Happy happy happy!

Oh, lots—

Way too many people.
Only…

REALLYREALLYFAST.
REALLYREALLYFAST.
REALLYREALLYREALLYREALLYREALLY
GO GO GO GO GO GO GO
STOP.

Selection
A-13

Rabbit Tango

¿Quieres sentir lo que es vivir?
El TANGO... *

D7   **Gm**

If there's a rab-bit, then you should grab it. Then you should grab it, gent-ly nab it, by the

D7   **A m6**

paws. And then sin-cere-ly you hold it near-ly as you a - wait the sud-den hush, and then ap-

D7   **Gm**

plause. Now with that rab-bit as if by ha-bit you be-gin that thril-ling dance a-cross the

D7   *rit.*   **Cm/E♭**   **E dim**   **D7/F♯**

floor, while in the hot light of your own spot-light there's a ma-gic that you ne-ver knew be-fore.

For *Bingo-Bango*!
It is a **TANGO!**
You hear the violins above
and bass beneath.
It is dramatic.
It's SO dramatic,
as the bunny holds a rose
between its
teeth.

¡Oh!—¿Quieres bailar?
Oh, la noche.
Oh, la música.
Ah si.
¡Ay!—¿Quieres soñar?
Las estrellas y un conejo
están aqui. **

(Do you want to dance?)

If! there's! a...rabbit,
then you should grab it.
Then you should grab it,
gently nab it, as it were.
But if there's not one,
you haven't got one,
and so the tango
that we spoke of
won't occur.

* Do you want to know what it means to live? The TANGO.

** Oh! Do you want to dance? O, the night! O, the music! Oh, yes!
Ah—Do you want to dream? The stars and a bunny are here.

A-15

When a Hippo Can Dance

Keep it going.

If you have a hippo you love very much, yet you find it has one or two faults—
such as sleeping too late, such as making you wait—I suggest that you teach it to waltz.
Now, there may be a lot of us who think "HIPPOPOTAMUS" and don't picture musical grace.
But just offer the chance to experience dance, and you may be surprised what takes place.

When a Hip-po Can Dance,   it's a thril-ling re-ve - la-tion. When a Hip-po Can Dance,   there is no-thing to say.

When a Hip-po Can Dance,   it's an o-ver-night sen - sa-tion.   Don't de-lay   teach your hip-po to-day. ___

But! Before you begin, here's a little advice,
and then we will see how it goes:
Though your hippo is sweet,
you've got to be fast with your feet,
or it might be quite hard on your toes. Zow!

When a Hippo Can Dance, it's a noble revelation.
When a Hippo Can Dance, there is nothing to say.
When a Hippo Can Dance, it's an overnight sensation.
Don't delay—teach your hippo today.

Now, if you are patient and practice a lot,
your hippo will surely improve.
And by April or May or ten years from today
how elegantly he will move!

I can see it now, you and your hippo,
blissfully gliding all over the stage.
I imagine how you dramatically dip, oh—
you and your hippo are all the rage.
𝕿𝖍𝖊 𝕹𝖊𝖜 𝖄𝖔𝖗𝖐 𝕿𝖎𝖒𝖊𝖘, front page!
Read all about it!

WHEN A HIPPO CAN DANCE!
When a Hippo Can Dance!
When a Hippo Can Dance…Dance…

When a Hippo Can Dance, it's a thrilling revelation.
When a Hippo Can Dance, there is NOTHING TO SAY!
When a Hippo Can Dance, it's an
overnight an overnight an overnight sensation.
Don't delay—teach your hippo today. Yeah.

Now there's just one thing that I
really ought to mention.
Just one thing that I've got to confess:
There may be a chance
that your hippo won't dance.
Well, it's a difficult thing to teach a hippo to swing.
It's unknown for their feet to connect with a beat.

No one who has tried it has had any success.
(At all. None whatsoever.)
In all recorded history, it's never been done.
We're counting on you to be the very first one.
We're counting on yoooooou! To be the very first one.

When a Hippo Can Dance, it's a thrilling revelation.
When a Hippo Can Dance, there is nothing to say.
When a Hippo Can Dance, it's an overnight sensation.
Don't delay—teach your hippo today…
Don't delay—teach your hippo today…

DON'T DELAY! TEACH YOUR HIPPO TODAY!

I like you a lot.
You're funny, and kind.
So let me explain
what I have in mind...

Your Personal Penguin

I want to   be Your Per - son - al Pen - guin. ___   I want to walk right by your __ side. __ I want to

be Your Per - son - al Pen   -   guin. ____   I want to trav el with you, far and ___ wide. ___   Wher-

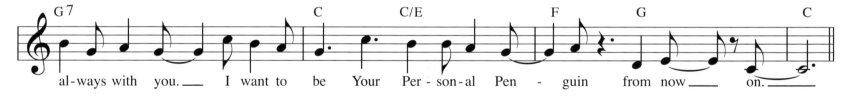

ev - er you go, ____   I'll   go there, ____ too. ____   Here and there and ev - 'ry - where and

al - ways with   you. ___   I want to   be   Your   Per - son - al   Pen   -   guin from now ___   on. ___

Now, lots of other penguins seem to do fine
in a universe of nothing but ice.
But if I could be yours,
and you could be mine,
our cozy little world would be twice as nice.

I want to be Your Personal Penguin.
I want to talk with you, night and day.
I want to be Your Personal Penguin.
I want to listen to whatever you say.

Look at these wings, so perfect to hold you.
I'd like to say again what I've already told you—
Let me be Your Personal Penguin from now on.

Now, lots of other penguins seem to do fine
in a universe of nothing but ice.
But if I could be yours, and you could be mine,
our cozy little world would be twice as nice.

I want to be (WANT TO BE!) Your Personal Penguin.
I want to walk right by your side.
I want to be (WANT TO BE!) Your Personal Penguin.
I want to travel with you, far and wide.
Wherever you go, I'll go there, too.
Here and there and everywhere
and always with you.
Please, may I be
Your Personal Penguin?

Imagine me,
Your Personal Penguin.
I want to be
YOUR PERSONAL PENGUIN
from now on!

*Please?
You're funny!
You're kind!*

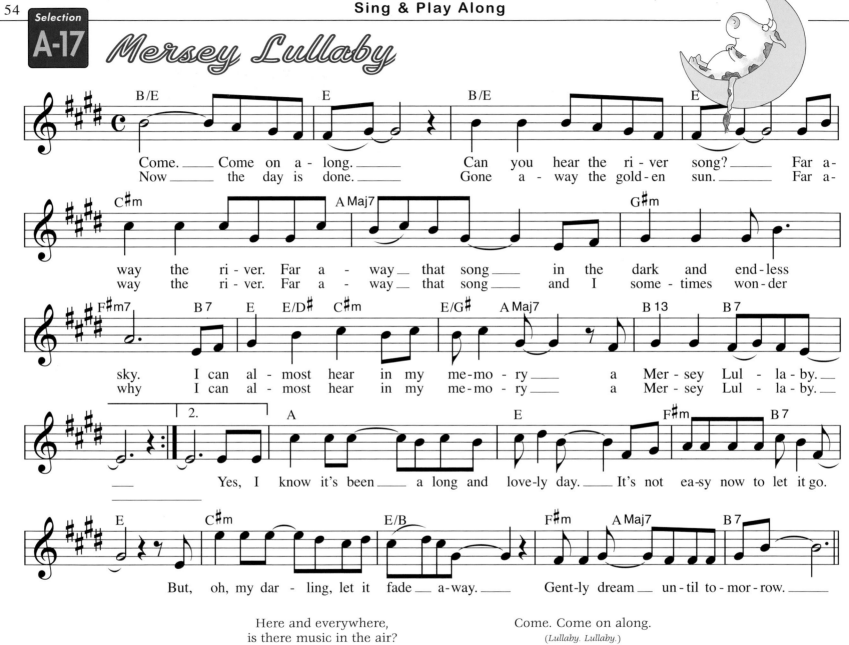

Selection A-17
Mersey Lullaby

B/E · E · B/E · E

Come. ___ Come on a - long. ___ Can you hear the ri - ver song? ___ Far a-
Now ___ the day is done. ___ Gone a - way the gold - en sun. ___ Far a-

C#m · A Maj7 · G#m

way the ri - ver. Far a - way ___ that song ___ in the dark and end - less
way the ri - ver. Far a - way ___ that song ___ and I some - times won - der

F#m7 · B7 · E · E/D# · C#m · E/G# · A Maj7 · B13 · B7

sky. I can al - most hear in my me - mo - ry ___ a Mer - sey Lul - la - by. ___
why I can al - most hear in my me - mo - ry ___ a Mer - sey Lul - la - by. ___

2. · A · E · F#m · B7

___ Yes, I know it's been ___ a long and love - ly day. ___ It's not eas - y now to let it go.

E · C#m · E/B · F#m · A Maj7 · B7

But, oh, my dar - ling, let it fade ___ a - way. ___ Gent - ly dream ___ un - til to - mor - row. ___

Here and everywhere,
is there music in the air?
Far away the river.
Far away that song
in the dark and endless sky.
May you always hear as you fall asleep
a Mersey Lullaby. A Mersey Lullaby.

Come. Come on along.
(Lullaby. Lullaby.)
Gone away the sun.
(Lullaby. Lullaby.)
Music everywhere.
(Lullaby. Lullaby.)
Oh—everywhere. Lullaby.

ABOUT THE SINGERS

THE SINGERS
in order of appearance

LAURA ROSE

CHRISTOPHER KALE JONES

Charismatic stage actor and singer of grace and subtlety. (Kale—pronounced "kah-lay"—is Hawaiian for Charles, Christopher's paternal grandfather's name.)

Best known for
his smart, edgy portrayal of the Four Seasons' Frankie Valli in the first national tour of the stunningly successful Broadway musical *Jersey Boys.*

Originally from
Oahu, Hawaii

GARY DE CAPU

SHA NA NA

Inimitable '50s rock-and-roll/comedy group, acclaimed and admired ever since their appearance at Woodstock.

Fluctuating membership. On this recording, they are:
JOCKO MARCELLINO tenor
REGGIE BATTISE bass
DONNY YORK baritone
SCREAMIN' SCOTT SIMON subtle presence
& MIKE FORD Honorary Sha

Best known for
their exuberant cuts on the *Grease* soundtrack, including "Those Magic Changes" "Rock & Roll Is Here to Stay" "Blue Moon" and "Tears on My Pillow." Screamin' Scott Simon wrote the lyrics for the song "Sandy."

Originally from
New York City
(Columbia University)

STEVE LAWRENCE

Sapphire-and-silver-voiced singer, and celebrated stage, film, and television actor. And, of course, partner of the so very wonderful Eydie Gorme.

Best known for
chart singles "Party Doll" (1957)
"Pretty Blue Eyes" (1959)
"Portrait of My Love" (1961)
"Go Away, Little Girl" (1963)
and many many many many albums.
Host of *The Steve Lawrence Show*, the last television show in black & white on CBS.

Originally from
Brooklyn, New York

Largely fictitious brass, vocal, and loud things ensemble, performing wherever the need is least. Playing relentlessly since, oh, let's say 1957.

Best known for
Not leaving.

JONATHAN DOSTER

THE UNINVITED LOUD PRECISION BAND
MICHAEL FORD, KEITH M. BOYNTON, DEVIN C.B. McEWAN,
MARK J. CAPECELATRO ESQ., GRAHAM LEONARD STONE, JAMES P. McEWAN

BRIAN WILSON
Lead singer/bassist of the exuberant Beach Boys; visionary, benevolent, and complex songwriter and music producer of great renown.

Best known for
an astounding 18 hit albums with more than 30 hit singles, including "Surfin'" (1962)
"409" (1962) "Surfin' USA" (1963) "Surfer Girl" (1963)
"Fun Fun Fun" (1964) "Don't Worry, Baby" (1964)
"I Get Around" (1964) "California Girls" (1965)
"Caroline, No" (1966) and "Wouldn't It Be Nice" (1966).

Originally from
Hawthorne, California

NEIL SEDAKA

Engaging and carefree singer, thoroughly captivating songwriter, and accomplished pianist.

Best known for

between 1960 and 1962, eight Top 40 hits: "The Diary" "Oh! Carol" "Stairway to Heaven" "Calendar Girl" "Little Devil" "Happy Birthday Sweet Sixteen" "Next Door to an Angel" and "Breaking Up Is Hard to Do"—all written by Sedaka with lyricist Howard Greenfield. Connie Francis had charted in 1958 with Sedaka/Greenfield's "Stupid Cupid," and in 1960 with the theme song for the MGM spring break classic *Where the Boys Are.*

Originally from Brooklyn, New York

THE SPARKLETS

Effervescent, smart and sophisticated girl group. All three Sparklets work afternoons at the malt shop.

DARCY M. BOYNTON lead vocal
MADELEINE LODGE high harmonies
KYLENE D. RAMOS low harmonies

Originally from
Hometown, USA

ELIZABETH ANDRIEN

JOHN ONDRASIK
of FIVE FOR FIGHTING

Cheerfully moody singer/songwriter/
pianist/guitarist, with a distinctive voice,
an inquisitive mind, and a '65 Mustang.

Originally from
The San Fernando Valley,
California

JIM WRIGHT

Best known for
hit singles
"Superman"
"100 Years"
"The Riddle"
and "World"
(*&* "Penguin Lament")

KEVIN WESTENBERG

B. B. KING

Yes, indeed, the King of the Blues. And a very nice man.

Best known for so many wonderful albums and bestselling singles,
among them "Three O'Clock Blues" (1951) "Woke Up This Morning" (1953)
"You Upset Me, Baby" (1954) "Every Day I Have the Blues" (1955)
"How Blue Can You Get?" (1963) and "The Thrill Is Gone" (1970).
His guitar, Lucille (photo left), is quite famous in her own right.

Originally from
Itta Bena, Mississippi

BOBBY VEE

Warm and wonderful teen idol,
Brill Building favorite, and musical
successor to the great Buddy Holly.

Best known for
many chart singles,
including
"Suzie Baby"
(1959, written by Vee)
"Take Good Care of
My Baby" (1961)
"Devil or Angel"
(1961)
"Rubber Ball" (1961)
"More Than I Can Say"
(1961)
"Run to Him" (1961)

Originally from
Fargo, North Dakota

MICHAEL FORD

Fabulous singer, pianist, composer, music producer, recording engineer, arranger, and all-around good guy.

Best known for
being the Ford half of the Boynton/Ford creative team on the albums *Rhinoceros Tap, Philadelphia Chickens,* and *Dog Train.*

Originally from
Philadelphia, Pennsylvania

JACK MITCHELL

PATTI LuPONE

Bold and bright Broadway legend, loved and admired for her astonishing range and versatility, both as an actress and as a singer.

Best known for
Broadway: *Evita* (Tony Award), *Anything Goes, Oliver!, Patti LuPone on Broadway, Master Class,* and *Noises Off.*
Encores! Series: *Pal Joey, Can-Can,* and *Gypsy.*
Royal Shakespeare: *Les Misérables* (Olivier Award). Numerous David Mamet plays and films.

Originally from
Northport, New York

KEITH BOYNTON

Singer, actor, playwright, filmmaker, man about town.

Best known for his strong yet sensitive rendition of "Be Like a Duck" on the cast album of the Unforgettable Imaginary Stage Spectacular, *Philadelphia Chickens.*

Originally from
The Berkshires

JAMIE McEWAN

DAVY JONES

Wry and adorable English-born actor, singer, jockey, and heartthrob; lead singer and fearless tambourinist of The Monkees.

Originally from
Manchester, England

Best known for
lead vocals on
"Daydream Believer" (1967)
"Valleri" (1967)
"I Wanna Be Free" (1967)
"A Little Bit Me, A Little Bit You" (1967)
"Girl" (1971)
Originated the role of
the Artful Dodger in *Oliver!*
on Broadway in 1962 (Tony nomination).

GERRY & THE PACEMAKERS

Ever-popular British Invasion merseybeat group, led by playful and boyish singer, songwriter, and guitarist Gerry Marsden.

Best known for
chart singles "How Do You Do It?" (1963) "I Like It" (1963) "You'll Never Walk Alone" (1963) and, written by Gerry Marsden: "I'm the One" (1964) "Don't Let the Sun Catch You Crying" (1964) and "Ferry Cross the Mersey" (1965).

Originally from Liverpool, England

JONATHAN DOSTER

DEVIN McEWAN

Understated and charming whitewater adventurer, dabbler in drumming, stealth crooner.

Recording Credits

Singing in the Shower **Christopher Kale Jones**
WORDS BY Sandra Boynton MUSIC BY Sandra Boynton & Michael Ford
BACKUP SINGERS Graham Stone, Michael Ford
LEAD RECORDED AT Capitol Studios, Hollywood, California
ENGINEER Chris Tergesen ASSISTANT Steve Genewick

Gorilla Song **Sha Na Na**
WORDS & MUSIC BY Sandra Boynton
VOCALS RECORDED AT Castle Oak Productions, Calabasas, California
ENGINEER Chris Tergesen ASSISTANT Josh Blanchard
HONORARY SHA Michael Ford

Blue Moo **Steve Lawrence**
WORDS & MUSIC BY Sandra Boynton
LEAD RECORDED AT Studio at the Palms, Las Vegas, Nevada
ENGINEER Chris Tergesen ASSISTANT Mark E. Gray
STRATOSPHERIC HARMONIES Beth Andrien
BACKUP SINGERS Michael Ford, Sandra Boynton

The Uninvited Parade / Return of the Uninvited Parade
The Uninvited Loud Precision Band
WORDS BY Sandra Boynton MUSIC BY Sandra Boynton & Michael Ford
RECORDED AT Studio Mike, Falls Village, Connecticut
ENGINEER Michael Ford

The Uninvited Parade Strikes Again
CREDITS AS ABOVE FOR *The Uninvited Parade*, PLUS STORE PERSONNEL
Beth Andrien, Michael Ford, Sandra Boynton

Speed Turtle **Brian Wilson**
WORDS & MUSIC BY Sandra Boynton
LEAD RECORDED AT Your Place or Mine
Glendale, California ENGINEER Mark Linett
*Brian Wilson's harmonies arranged and
recorded by* Brian Wilson
MORE HARMONIES Graham Stone,
Devin McEwan, Michael Ford

Your Nose **Neil Sedaka**
WORDS BY Sandra Boynton MUSIC BY
Sandra Boynton & Neil Sedaka
LEAD RECORDED AT Avatar Studios,
New York ENGINEER Chris Tergesen
ASSISTANT Justin Gerrish
STRATOSPHERIC HARMONIES Beth Andrien

Blue Moo '62 **The Sparklets**
WORDS & MUSIC BY Sandra Boynton
RECORDED AT Studio Mike,
Falls Village, Connecticut
ENGINEER Michael Ford

Big Band Sound **John Ondrasik of Five for Fighting**
WORDS BY Sandra Boynton MUSIC BY Sandra Boynton & Michael Ford
LEAD RECORDED AT WorldBeat Recording, Calabasas, California
ENGINEER Chris Tergesen ASSISTANT Aurin Lahiri
VINTAGE RECORDING CLIPS BY the Fordtones & Beth Andrien
John Ondrasik appears courtesy of Aware/Columbia Records

One Shoe Blues **B.B. King** WORDS & MUSIC BY Sandra Boynton
LEAD RECORDED AT Avatar Studios, New York
VOCAL & GUITAR ENGINEER Roy Hendrickson ASSISTANT Chad Lupo
B.B. King appears courtesy of Geffen Records

With You **Bobby Vee**
WORDS & MUSIC BY Sandra Boynton
RECORDED AT Rockhouse Productions Studio, St. Joseph, Minnesota
ENGINEER Jeff Engholm ASSISTANT Jordan Reichle
UPRIGHT BASS Tommy Vee DRUMS Jeff Vee GUITAR Danny Neale
BACKUP SINGERS Michael Ford, Graham Stone, Sandra Boynton

Loud!/Quiet **Michael Ford**
WORDS BY Sandra Boynton MUSIC BY Sandra Boynton & Michael Ford
RECORDED AT Studio Mike, Falls Village, Connecticut
ENGINEER Michael Ford
HALLELUJAH CHORUS Rachel Ford, Katie Ford

Rabbit Tango **Patti LuPone**
WORDS BY Sandra Boynton MUSIC BY Sandra Boynton & Michael Ford
RECORDED AT Studio Mike, Falls Village, Connecticut
ENGINEER Michael Ford
TANGO INSTRUCTOR Señor John McMullan

When a Hippo Can Dance **Keith Boynton**
WORDS BY Sandra Boynton MUSIC BY Sandra Boynton & Michael Ford
RECORDED AT Studio Mike, Falls Village, Connecticut
ENGINEER Michael Ford STRATOSPHERIC HARMONIES Beth Andrien

Your Personal Penguin **Davy Jones**
WORDS & MUSIC BY Sandra Boynton
LEAD RECORDED AT Carriage House Studios, Stamford, Connecticut
ENGINEER Chris Tergesen ASSISTANTS John Montagnese, Russ Hoppe
BASS HIPPO Michael Ford

Mersey Lullaby **Gerry & the Pacemakers**
WORDS & MUSIC BY Sandra Boynton
LEAD RECORDED AT Avatar Studios, New York
ENGINEER Brian Montgomery ASSISTANT Colin Suzuki

It's Not Over **Devin McEwan and the U.L.P.B.**
WORDS BY Sandra Boynton MUSIC BY Sandra Boynton & Michael Ford
RECORDED AT Studio Mike, Falls Village, Connecticut
ENGINEER Michael Ford

& Thank-yous

JAMIE McEWAN *He's sure the boy I love* —SKB
BETH ANDRIEN *The sweetest voice in my life* —MF
CAITLIN & KEITH & DEVIN & DARCY
and RACHEL & JOHN & KATIE
the greatest kids imaginable

Terrific Family & Friends
Jeanne Boynton, Aunt Ruth
Nancy, Danny, Judy, Kathy, Debbie,
Pam, Susie, Patty, Sherry, Laurie &
Alison Boynton, and Dick, Barb, Lynn, Doug
& Kim Mackay, Alberta Donaldson
Ash & Kyle Boynton, Em & Robb Stey
John Stey, Carl Yeich
Jackie Tintle, Linda & Dara Epstein
McEwans, Markoffs, Hansons & Sedgwicks
David Allender, the Biaginis, the Binzens
the Capecelatros, Steve Callahan &
Randy Dwenger, the Clarkes, Robin Corey
James Creque, Mike & Beth Ford
Sarah Getz, Frank Grusauskas &
Trudy Schaelchli, Paul Hanson
the Keisers, the Kirbers
Billy J. Kramer & Roni Ashton
Laura Linney, Patti LuPone
Brian & Renée Mann
Gerry & Pauline Marsden
Kelley Merwin, Susan Mieras, the Ondrasiks
Danny Peary & Suzanne Rafer
Nora & Bob Rivkin, the Sherrills
Susan Spano, the Stanleys
Christine Stevens, Graham Stone
Skip Strobel, Chris Tergesen & Toni Lewis
all the Workmans, the Yankovics
Gina & Bruce Young
—and also from Mike:
Pat & Marlene, Lucyann & John
the Andriens, Carl Kusnell, Steve Black
Sandy & Jamie, Noel Heagerty
Dick Lolla & Paula Pierce

Home Front
Kathleen Sherrill aka "The Governethel"
Ken Kizilski/FEDEX
Lisa Hoage, Jill Thomen & Billie Martocchio
  /LAKEVILLE POST OFFICE
Jean Bell/JEAN BELL TRAVEL
Matt Schwartz
Ken Chase & Jay d'Andrea, Sheila Hough

Fine Music Biz People
David Ankrum & Teresa Wolf
  /SCHIOWITZ CONNOR ANKRUM WOLF
Rob Cohen/SONY/AWARE
Dean Egnater/APEX ARTS
Jim Grant/LITTLE BIG MAN PRODUCTIONS
Susan Jacobs/SONY/BMG
Floyd Lieberman, Tina France/LIEBERMAN ENT.
Joseph Lilak/WILLIAM MORRIS
Jocko Marcellino/SHA NA NA
John Owen/CAPITOL/EMI
Robert Pratt & Mary Connell/ROYAL CHIMES LTD.
Deborah Robicheau/DAVID JONES ENTERTAINMENT
Robert Scott/ROJON PRODUCTIONS
Leba Sedaka & Robert Cotto &
Lui Marquez/NEIL SEDAKA MUSIC
Jean Sievers/THE LIPPIN GROUP
Judy Tannen/CONCORD PRODUCTIONS
LaVerne Toney/B.B. KING'S OFFICE
Jeff Velline/ROCKHOUSE PRODUCTIONS
Melinda Wilson
Dee Dee Wright/GEFFEN RECORDS
Lisa Zahn/NARAS

Critical Technical Advice & Studio Support
Dan Timmons/GLYPH TECHNOLOGIES
Mark Bruhn/SWEETWATER
David Maffucci/VISIONARY COMPUTERS
Mark Linett/YOUR PLACE OR MINE
Paula Salvatore/CAPITOL RECORDING
Chris Tergesen
Zoe Thrall/STUDIO AT THE PALMS

Visual Ingenuity
Terry Bob Cratchit Ortolani/PINT-SIZE PRODUCTIONS
Beth Andrien/BETH ANDRIEN VIDEOGRAPHY
Rachel Ford/RACHEL FORD DESIGNS
Robert Alessi
Bill Binzen/BILL BINZEN PHOTOGRAPHY
Jonathan Doster/JONATHAN DOSTER PHOTOGRAPHY
Jon DePreter/DEPRETER DESIGNS
Jack Lawton/LAWTON DRUM COMPANY
John Rivard & Jennifer Hetherington
  /SALON DAVID GAVIN

Kind and Helpful People
Peter Bunetta, Pam Ortolani
Jane & Mark Capecelatro
Lauren Caracciolo/MERRILL LYNCH
The incredible staff/ST. REGIS HOTEL, NYC
The fabulous folks/SHUTTERS OF SANTA MONICA
Ann Getsinger, Christine Gray
Stephanie Plunkett & everyone at
THE NORMAN ROCKWELL MUSEUM
Rob Nellson/SALISBURY CENTRAL MUSIC DEPT.
Esmeralda Soufan, Ezra Velazquez

Davy Jones
Jenny Mandel
Frank Caruso
& KING FEATURES
Nancy Davis
Kimberly DesJardine
Bryan Gonzalvo
eBay
John McMullan
Herb Prem
Ian Sambor
Cathy Sherrill
Ronald Viafore/
KENT CENTER SCHOOL
and all the
wonderful
Vees
!

Book Credits & Thank-yous

...and that was, of course, everybody's favorite teen, Neil Sedaka—here on WKOW, the #1 AM radio rock-and-roll station in this rock-and-roll nation. We have some important thank-yous going out now. First, to **SUZANNE RAFER.** Suzi Q, what a wise and amazing editor you are. Thank you for all that you do. And next, coming all the way from Buffalo, incredible designer and layout technician, **TERRY ORTOLANI.** Terry, it really couldn't have happened without your wonderful work. You are absolutely positively the very best. Thanks also to the swell art department at Workman Publishing. You know who you are—**HARRY SCHRODER, SUE McLEOD, CYNTHIA GARCIA-VEGAS,** and **PHILIP HOFFHINES.** And, wow, those Novellus Graphics people way up in Toronto! **RON, SHAWN & MICHAEL RICKETTS, CHRISTINE ANTONSEN, WAYNE BOOTH, ANDREW BENT,** and **DAVID McMULLEN!** Bravo! Production at Workman is calmly and expertly handled by none other than **WAYNE KIRN.** A great big thank-you goes to you, Wayne. And what would copy-editing be without the sharp eyes of the terrific **IRENE DEMCHYSHYN**? And how about that music typesetting? Hey, **BRUCE JOHNSON,** take a bow! Publicity and marketing folks, great great work. That's you, **KIM SMALL, AMY CORLEY,** **PAGE EDMUNDS,** and **PETE BOHAN.** Endless thanks to the fabulous **JENNY MANDEL,** and to the coolest book publisher on the planet, namely **PETER WORKMAN.**

And now, the weather.

HEY, LOOK! *It's an easy Do-it-Yourself Project!*

FOLD →

To make a nifty jewel case insert for your **BLUE MOO** Compact Disc, simply cut where indicated, then fold the 2 side flaps inward. Take it to the drive-in, the sock hop, Hillson's Soda Fountain—wherever the hep kids are going after school.

(Though honestly, the technology for this whole "compact disc" idea won't really be ready till near the end of the 20th century.)

FOLD →

CUT HERE
VERTICALLY

10. ONE SHOE BLUES
B.B. King

11. WITH YOU Bobby Vee

12. LOUD!/QUIET Michael Ford

13. RABBIT TANGO
Patti LuPone

14. THE UNINVITED PARADE
STRIKES AGAIN
The Uninvited Loud Precision Band

15. WHEN A HIPPO CAN
DANCE
Keith Boynton

16. YOUR
PERSONAL PENGUIN
Davy Jones of the Monkees

17. MERSEY LULLABY
Gerry & the Pacemakers

18. IT'S NOT OVER
HIDDEN TRACK
Devin McEwan & The U.L.P.B.

17 Jukebox Hits from Way Back Never

Lyrics by **SANDRA BOYNTON** Music by **BOYNTON & FORD**

Blue Moo

B.B. KING
BOBBY VEE
BRIAN WILSON
THE UNINVITED LOUD PRECISION BAND
CHRISTOPHER KALE JONES
DAVY JONES
DEVIN McEWAN
GERRY & THE PACEMAKERS
JOHN ONDRASIK
KEITH BOYNTON
MICHAEL FORD
NEIL SEDAKA
PATTI LuPONE
SHA NA NA
THE SPARKLETS
STEVE LAWRENCE

1. SINGING IN THE SHOWER
Christopher Kale Jones

2. GORILLA SONG
Sha Na Na

3. BLUE MOO
Steve Lawrence

4. THE UNINVITED PARADE
The Uninvited Loud Precision Band

5. RETURN OF THE
UNINVITED PARADE
The Uninvited Loud Precision Band

6. SPEED TURTLE
Brian Wilson

7. YOUR NOSE
Neil Sedaka

8. BLUE MOO '62
The Sparklets

9. BIG BAND SOUND
John Ondrasik of Five For Fighting

$\mathcal{M}$usic production, instrumental arrangement, demos,
vocal comping, and mixing of all songs
(not to mention many zesty claps, snaps, and gratuitous percussive events)
done at Studio Mike, Falls Village, Connecticut
by Michael Ford and Sandra Boynton

———

Mr. Ford performs nearly every single one
of the instruments you hear on all the tracks*

———

Recording sessions take place at the recording studio
most convenient to the singer
Sessions are prepared by Mike, and
directed by Sandy, with music direction by Mike**

———

Mastered at Sterling Sound, New York City
MASTERING ENGINEER Chris Gehringer

———

Album produced by Sandra Boynton

* the Vees play guitar, drums & bass on "With You"
  and B.B. King plays guitar on "One Shoe Blues"

** Brian Wilson ran his own session for "Speed Turtle"